FUN THINGS TO DO WITH GRANDKIDS

You have the best job in the world...being a grandma! Whether they call you Nana, Mimi, Gigi, Granny, Mammaw, or another name, there is no more special name than the one you are called by your grandkids. Make your times together as fun and meaningful as you can by storing up on the treasure chest of ideas right in this book. You'll find simple ways to explore your neighborhood, celebrate the natural world, make awesome art activities, play, act, create, eat ... And then take some quiet time for watching clouds, blowing bubbles, and sharing stories.

Enjoy every minute!

Grandparents, always carefully supervise your grandchildren when enjoying these activities together, especially around water, in the kitchen, or when using sharp objects. Remember that any activity involving small parts can present a choking hazard and is not suitable for children under the age of 3. Before beginning any activity, take into consideration your grandchildren's ages, abilities, and any allergies they may have, and adapt your plans accordingly. Stay safe and have fun!

Fun Things to do With Grandkids; ISBN 978-0-9991681-9-6
Published by Product Concept Mfg., Inc., 2175 N. Academy Circle #201, Colorado Springs, CO 80909
©2018 Product Concept Mfg., Inc. All rights reserved.
Written and Compiled by Vicki J. Kuyper and Joanne Mattern in association with Product Concept Mfg., Inc.

Hosting a Grandma Camp is a wonderful opportunity to build a deeper relationship with your grandkids by spending an extended time together. It's also a great way to care for your own grown children, by giving them some time and space alone without the kids.

A good length of time to give your grandkids a real "going to camp" feel is three to seven days. If both parents work outside the home, scheduling Grandma Camp over a school break can also offer a short-time alternative to day care. Try and include as many of your grandchildren as your living space can hold. Allowing cousins to hang out together not only helps them grow closer, but often gives you a bit of a break, because they'll enjoy the novelty of hanging out with other kids. However, the number of grandkids you invite, the time of year, length of the camp, and elaborateness of the activities you schedule is totally up to you! Only commit to what your time, space, finances, and energy level can handle.

SETTING UP CAMP

Setting up suitable sleeping arrangements is vitally important. Sleep-deprived grandkids—or grandmas—do not make happy campers. Carefully consider your grandchildren's ages and sleep habits. Have grandkids bring their own sleeping bags, if possible. If the weather is nice, pitch a tent in the backyard. A great alternative for younger children is to use a child safe pop-up castle or play-house indoors.

Have an individual cubby (which could be a laundry basket, box, or laundry bag) ready for each child. Explain that this is where they keep all of their personal belongings, so shoes and socks, etc., don't get mixed up. This also helps keep the kid clutter to a minimum.

Prepare a backpack for each grandchild. Put in a new toothbrush, necessary toiletries, a disposable camera, and a small stuffed animal (for younger kids) or journal and fun pen or pencil (for older kids). You may even want to include a Grandma Camp t-shirt. Purchase inexpensive, solid color t-shirts and write the name of each grandchild on them in fabric paint or iron-on letters. Or, have each child choose a special "camp" name and then have them decorate the shirts as a camp project. Afterwards, campers can use their backpacks to bring home any special trinkets and projects they've made during their time with you.

When everyone arrives, have a camp meeting, so the kids will know what to expect. Talk about all of the fun you're going to have—and give a simple list of camp rules. Remember to include rules, such as "Be kind to each other," "Clean up your own mess," etc.

*Unless you want to set up a special movie night, try and keep Grandma Camp a Screen-Free Zone! No television, cell phones, video games, or internet surfing. Make this a special time to connect with real, live people.

THEMES

Although simply enjoying time together is the real theme of every Grandma Camp, it can be fun to set a theme for the entire camp stay or choose a different theme for each day. Here are a few theme ideas worth considering: superheroes, science, animals, a favorite kids' book or movie, different countries of the world or periods in history. Tie each day's activities and menu into your theme. You may even want to do a bit of quick and easy decorating!

ACTIVITIES

Obviously, the potential for fun-filled camp activities are endless! Any of the ideas included in this book would be a great place to start. Carefully consider your individual campers' ages and interests as you plan your time together. Include a little bit of something for everybody. Don't over plan your day, but keep several extra ideas in mind, just in case one activity doesn't connect well with your campers or unfavorable weather forces a change of plans. You may want to schedule a period of Quiet Time each day, when kids sit on their sleeping bags and read a book, draw, or think up a story in their head that they can share with the group later. This is a great time for those who still need a nap to take one. Also, don't forget to allow free time for the grandkids to simply play together in the backyard or at a park.

BELATED BIRTHDAYS

If your grandkids do not live close to you, you may have missed the joy of celebrating their birthdays with them in person. If this is the case, why not celebrate belated birthdays at Grandma Camp? You could celebrate one child each day or simply have one big party that celebrates everyone.

BED TIME

Sleeping in a new place can be a tough transition for children, especially the younger ones. You can make it easier by setting a nighttime camp routine in place.

- First, make sure you're familiar with what your grandkids' regular bedtime routines are at home and try to stick as closely to them—and to their usual bedtimes—as possible.

- If your day is going to involve caffeine, sugar, or big meals, plan them for earlier in the day.

- Make sure your grandkids are warm enough, or cool enough, before it's time for lights out.

- Have a transition time, where you plan quieter activities, for the hour before bedtime.

- Have a grandkid story time. You come up with the first sentence, then go around in a circle with every child adding one sentence to create an original bedtime story.

- If a child is having difficulty sleeping, sit close to him or her and breathe deeply in sync with each other. Like yawning, it's contagious, and can help calm an anxious little heart.

CAMP TIME TREATS

It wouldn't be camp without special treats, including s'mores! If your grandkids aren't old enough to toast marshmallows around the fire, or you don't have a fireplace or outside firepit, here are some quick and easy alternatives:

S'MORES FOR A CROWD

Preheat the oven to 400 degrees. Line a baking sheet with parchment paper. Unroll a tube of purchased crescent roll dough onto the paper. Pinch the seams together and fold up the edges of the rectangular sheet of dough to form a short crust. Combine 1 1/2 Tbsp. of sugar and 1/2 tsp. of cinnamon in a bowl and then sprinkle over the dough. Bake crust 10 to 15 minutes or until golden brown. Remove baking sheet from oven and top with six, 9.3 oz chocolate bars. Cover with one bag of large marshmallows. Return to oven for about 10 minutes. Watch carefully and remove as soon as the marshmallows melt and turn brown. Cut into 12 servings.

MICROWAVE S'MORES

Put 1/2 of a graham cracker on a microwaveable plate. Top with a large square of chocolate and a large marshmallow. Microwave on high 15 to 20 seconds, or until marshmallow puffs. Top with another graham cracker. Let cool for a minute. Eat!

BREAKFAST CEREAL BUFFET PARFAITS

For a quick and easy breakfast for a crowd, set out a variety of boxes of breakfast cereal and granola, as well as raisins, dried cranberries, raspberries, blueberries, coconut, and plain yogurt. Have grandkids layer their parfait ingredients in a disposable, clear plastic cup.

HOMEMADE ICE CREAM SANDWICHES

Bake refrigerated cookie dough according to the directions on the package. Scoop ice cream into a hamburger patty press. Put one round of ice cream between two cooled cookies and enjoy.

TRAIL MIX BUFFET

Let kids prepare their own bags of trail mix for a trip to the park—or simply to carry with them as they play in the backyard. Give each grandkids a small, resealable plastic bag and then have them add whatever they'd like from a buffet of ingredients, such as: breakfast cereal, gummy bears, nuts, raisins, candy-coated chocolates candies, goldfish crackers). Adjust as needed if your grandkids or invited cousins are allergic to gluten or nuts.

WRAP IT UP!

Turn those happy camper memories into the perfect Christmas gift by making a photo album for each family with images of your time together. It's one way to make Grandma Camp last year-round.

BREATHING ROOM

Remember to give yourself some time to relax before, during, and after camp. When the kids head to bed, head to the bathtub or read a magazine. Don't use every spare minute preparing or cleaning up. A little bit of breathing room for you can help make Grandma Camp a much more enjoyable experience for you, one you'll want to repeat year-after-year.

WRITE YOUR FIRST BOOK

Kids love looking at pictures of themselves! This year, bypass the usual toy store Christmas or birthday gifts. Use candid shots of your grandkids from your phone (or ask their parents to email you some recent vacation photos) and have those snapshots made into a board book your grandkids can enjoy for years to come. There are many photo book/board book companies available on the internet that you can choose from. Simply click and drag your photos into their format. You can even type in a personalized story about the photos, if you wish. If your grandchild is just learning to read, keep it simple. For instance, "G is for Grandma" belongs right below a picture of you!

Riddle Dee Dee

Where is the best place to see a man-eating fish?

CALLING ALL LITTLE ARTISTS AND AUTHORS!

Make a keepsake for both grandkids and their parents, by scanning kids' artwork and having it made into a "photo" album through an online service. You can also have your grandkids draw pictures to help illustrate a favorite bedtime story or write an original story of their own.

THINGS TO DO WITH AN

ICE CREAM CONE!

Plant seeds in a cake cone. Its flat bottom makes it a fairly stable miniature garden. After the seeds sprout they are easily transplanted to the garden. Put the entire cone in the ground. It's biodegradable!

Half-fill cake cones with cake batter. Grandma will bake at the temperature recommended for cupcakes. After they cool, top with a squirt of canned whipped cream. It's an instant party without the need for plates and forks.

Fill cake or sugar cones with rice cereal treats. These are just as tasty as the original but keep little hands from getting overly sticky.

For an easy-to-eat picnic treat, fill cake cones with tuna or chicken salad. Wrap in plastic wrap. They are easy to hold and eat!

Instead of cannoli, try a CONE-oli! Roll the tips of sugar cones in melted dark chocolate. Then roll in mini-chocolate chips. After it has set, fill each cone with your favorite ricotta cannoli mixture.

Make a bird feeder! Use a pencil to poke a hole in the pointed end of a sugar cone. Knot the end of a pipe cleaner. Thread the pipe cleaner through the hole, with the knot inside the cone. Spread peanut butter on the outside of the cone and then roll it in birdseed. Use the exposed pipe cleaner to attach the bird feeder to a tree branch, preferably one your grandkids can easily see.

Turn sugar cones into Christmas trees. Cover with green frosting. Decorate with breakfast cereal, nuts, shredded coconut, sprinkles, and small candies.

FEED THE BIRDIES!

MILK JUG FEEDER

You will need:

- Gallon milk jug
- Scissors
- Twine
- Sticks
- Glue or sturdy tape
- Craft paint
- Stickers

1. Wash and dry the milk jug. Remove the cap.
2. Cut windows in the larger sides of the jug.
3. Use the scissor to punch holes near the top of the jug. (It's best to have an adult do this step!)
4. String twine through the holes so your bird feeder can hang up.
5. Add a perch by gluing or taping sticks to the feeder holes.
6. Decorate your feeder with craft paint, stickers, or whatever you like.
7. Fill with bird seed.
8. Hang your feeder in a tree near the window so you can watch your bird friends enjoy their treats!

PINECONE FEEDER

This is especially fun for kids when winter's on its way, and the sparrows, cardinals, and other birds will need sustenance for the cold days ahead. Go on a nature scavenger hunt, finding pine cones of all sizes to use as birdfeeder structures. Spread the pinecones with peanut butter, then sprinkle with birdseed. Tie yarn to the top of each and hang it from a tree as a gift to our feathered friends.

WATERMELON IMPOSTER!

When watermelon isn't in season, you can still have a summery treat that's easy to make and fun to eat. Set one container of lime sherbet, and one of raspberry, on the counter until slightly softened. Coat the inside of a large plastic bowl with spray-on vegetable oil. Spread the lime sherbet around the inside of the bowl, about an inch thick. Mix miniature chocolate chips into the raspberry sherbet. Fill the lime "rind" with the raspberry sherbet mixture. Return to the freezer and let harden. When ready to serve, turn the "melon" out of the plastic bowl. Cut into slices like a real melon. Enjoy your faux fruit treat!

BACKYARD WATER PARK

Though heading to a water park can be a lot of fun, the crowds, travel time, and expense, can make the outing less appealing. Why not make your own water slide at home? Secure an old shower curtain, plastic tablecloth, or trash bags on an open space of lawn. Use tent hooks, rocks, or bricks to hold your slide in place. Turn the hose on the "spray" setting and set it on the edge of your slide, with the water flowing down lengthwise. Slip and slide for about 1/2 hour in one spot before moving your water park to another area of the yard, so you won't damage the lawn.

Tongue Twister

Soldier's Shoulders
Soldier's Shoulders
Soldier's Shoulders

EMOTIONAL ARTWORK

Talking freely about our emotions is important at any age, but here's one way to help your grandchildren better express what they're feeling through art. Give each child several pieces of paper (or paper plates) and crayons or markers. Then, talk about one emotion at a time, such as joy, anger, fear, excitement, sadness, loneliness, envy, disappointment, etc. Discuss different situations where they're likely to experience these emotions—even if they're unfamiliar with the exact word used to describe how they feel. Ask them to draw a picture expressing how that emotion feels. It may be abstract, a specific scene, or a face expressing that emotion. Label each drawing with its corresponding emotion. Hang the completed artwork in their bedroom. When an emotional situation arises, take your grandchild into his or her room and ask them which picture shows how they're feeling right now. Their own artwork is a great conversation starter, especially when emotions threaten to run amuck! You can also use this project to help grandkids better understand how YOU are feeling during emotional situations.

Riddle Dee Dee

What can sit in a corner and yet travel around the world?

MESS-FREE PAINTING

Kids love to create with water soluable paint. Save some of the mess and expense by simply using water. Give your grandkids a brush and a bucket of water and let them paint the sidewalk, wooden fence, or stucco. To paint inside, fill a small squirt bottle with water and let them "paint" a picture on craft paper. Just be sure to put newspaper beneath their artwork—and be prepared for a few random squirts to "accidentally" splash on their siblings.

MAGAZINE MESSAGES

Help your grandkids with their reading skills by making random sentences out of words cut from old magazines. Or try making a scene from a collage of magazine pictures—and then piece together a story that goes with the picture from the words available.

MIXED UP MENAGERIE

Using old magazines, cut out pictures of faces, legs, arms, etc. from people and animals. Then, have your grandkids glue them together in crazy ways.

MAKE YOUR OWN CHIPS

Spray 6" corn tortillas with vegetable-oil cooking spray on both sides. Sprinkle with salt or cinnamon sugar, if desired. Stack tortillas and cut into quarters. Spread the tortillas on a cookie sheet and bake for 8 to 10 minutes, at 350° until crisp and lightly browned.

JUST SAY CHEESE!

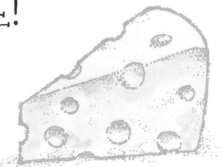

Grilled cheese is always a lunchtime favorite. Add some extra pizazz to mealtime at Grandma's by letting the kids create their own tasty combinations, and when their masterpieces are ready Grandma can grill them on the stove.

Try one of these tasty combos.

- Fig jam, sliced turkey, baby spinach, and Havarti.
- Bacon, thinly sliced green apple, and sharp cheddar.
- Brie, fig jam, and thinly sliced apple.
- Macaroni and cheese grilled between two slices of French bread.
- Favorite pizza toppings, provolone cheese, and garlic bread, with marinara dipping sauce.
- Smashed avocado, bacon, and gouda cheese.
- Cinnamon raisin bread, brie, and orange marmalade.
- Hazelnut spread and banana.
- Ham, crushed pineapple, jack cheese, and a brush of teriyaki sauce.
- Cheddar cheese, bacon, and apple butter, between two frozen waffles (thaw before grilling)
- Sliced hot dog "rings" and American cheese. Serve with ketchup and mustard.
- Taco seasoned ground beef, crushed corn chips, tomatoes, and cotija cheese.

For extra fun: use cookie cutters to cut your finished sandwiches into interesting, easy-to hold-shapes (such as stars, hearts, or "gingerbread" people). Around the holidays, try Christmas trees or Easter eggs.

TABLETOP FOOTBALL

Play football with a small piece of paper folded into a triangle. All you need is a sheet of notebook paper.

1. Fold the paper in half lengthwise to make a long skinny rectangle.
2. Repeat two more times, so you have an even skinnier, long rectangle.
3. Starting at the top right corner, fold the corner down into a triangle shape.
4. Continue to fold the paper down into triangles.
5. Tuck the last piece into the fold to complete your football.

Play by flicking the football with your fingers. Your opponent places his or her fists on the table to create the goal posts.

CAN YOU SOLVE IT?

Create word puzzles. Choose a theme and think of words related to that theme. Themes could be animals, foods, people from the Bible, things that smell icky, for examples. Scramble the letters, write down each word, and challenge your grandkids to figure them out.

Riddle Dee Dee

What do you call a boomerang that doesn't work?

NATURE'S TREASURES

Enjoy a day outside! Notice all the unique colors, shapes, and textures you can see... flower petals, feathers, leaves, seed pods, acorns, stones, shells. Gather them and create a memory mobile by hanging them on a rod or tree limb with wire, string, or twine!

STAINED GLASS WINDOW HANGINGS

You don't have to play with shards of glass to get a piece of art that resembles "stained glass." Have your grandchildren outline a scene in permanent black marker or with a black ink pen on a piece of white paper. Then have them color the rest of the picture with bright-colored crayons. Turn the drawing over and lay it on newspaper, several sheets thick. With an old rag, rub a small amount of baby oil or cooking oil all over the back of the picture. When the picture dries, hang it in a window or on a sliding glass door. The picture will be transparent!

FURRY FRIENDS

Visit an animal shelter with your animal-loving grandchild. Better yet, volunteer at one! Animals waiting for a home will appreciate your love and attention.

NATURE'S CLOSE-UP

Go on a photo scavenger hunt at the park. Give each child a disposable camera and a list of items to find and photograph. If they're not yet old enough to read, use stickers for easy-to-find items, such as leaves, rocks, a ladybug, a cat, a tree, shoes (which will remind them to look at their own feet!), a bird, clouds, a slide, another child—and a grandma! Develop or download the photos, and then have your grandkids use them to make a collage.

MAKE A KITE FROM A BAG

You will need:

- Long, thin sticks
- A trash bag
- A ball of string
- Scissors
- Tape
- Ribbon

1. Use the string to tie the sticks together in the shape of a cross. Use tape to reinforce the string and make your kite stronger.
2. Cut the garbage bag to fit around the four points of your kite. Tie the bag to every point and lightly tape the edges.
3. Flip your kite over and tie a piece of string across the middle of the kite. Make sure it has a little slack.
4. Take your ball of string and tie it to the other stick to form a triangle in the cross section of the kite. That same string will then be tied to the other string. It should now resemble a pyramid when it is pulled taut.
5. Add a ribbon to the bottom of your kite.
6. Take your kite outside on a windy day and let it fly!

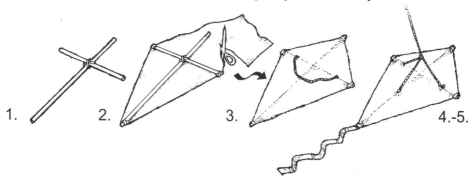

1.   2.   3.   4.-5.

OOH LA LA!

Take a trip to a foreign country without leaving your living room! All it takes is a bit of preparation beforehand. How much work you put into it is totally up to you. Here are a few ideas to get you started:

- Watch a short DVD travelogue rented from the library, on the internet, or read a storybook set in the country you are going to "travel" to. If you've personally visited your chosen country before, look through a photo album of yours together.

- Talk about what you would need to travel to your chosen country and help your grandkids pack a few things in a backpack—then pretend to fly, sail, or travel by train to your destination.

- Talk about famous sites you'd see at your destination and let your grandkids plan the day's imaginary itinerary.

- Can you think of any famous people born in this country? Tell your grandkids about them.

- Practice using a few words, like "hello," "good-bye," and "thank you" in your chosen country's native language.

- Don't forget snacks! Pick up a few exotic treats at an ethnic market or make a meal together, such as crepes, quesadillas, scones, bratwurst, or baklava.

- Make plans to travel together some day in the future! Make a travel piggy bank.

MAKESHIFT TRIP TO THE SEA

Place a handful of shells you've collected, or purchased, in a mesh laundry bag. Add a book about seashells that can help your grandchild identify the shells in the bag.

GRANNY SAYS!

This version of Simon Says can make cleaning up or getting ready for bed more fun! Whether you're Granny, Grandma, Meemaw, Nana, or whatever clever moniker you're known by, help your grandkids accomplish what needs to be done by mixing in a little silliness. For instance, try this: "Granny says take off one shoe. Granny says hop on one foot. Take off the other shoe. Granny says take off your sister's shoe. Put that shoe on your foot." See how quickly you can get the giggles going!

Riddle Dee Dee

What do you call a funny book about eggs?

GIGGLES AND GRINS!

For this game, all you need is a tissue (or a piece of paper or bandana)—and some giggly grandkids. Explain they can laugh and giggle as long as the paper is in the air, but as soon as it hits the ground they have to freeze. Not only can they no longer make any sound, they can't even smile! If they do, during the next round they get to make funny faces at whoever is left playing to try and make them laugh, as well.

PUZZLES & GAMES!

Place small objects in a bag or a bucket of sand. Try to identify each object just by feel and without looking at it.

Create a secret code and send each other messages. Substitute numbers for letters, or a different letter for each letter. For example, A=1, B=2, or A=Z, B=Y, etc.

Have a color hunt. Choose a color and see how many things you find that are that color. You can play this game inside or outside.

Wrap ordinary objects in paper and have the child guess what each object is without opening it. Have the last object be a special surprise, such as a new toy or game.

Have a dance party! Put in a CD or find some lively music on the radio or the computer and dance up a storm!

Play True or False. Write down five sentences about yourself. Four are true but one is not. See if your grandchild can guess which statement is not true. Then switch places.

Make a fort by draping sheets over the furniture. Line the inside with pillows. Curl up inside with a good book and a snack.

SUPER SLEUTH

Like snowflakes, every person (including grand-kids and grandmas!) is a one-of-a-kind creation. Helping our grandkids understand this fact can help them become more sensitive to differences in the people around them. Use this fingerprint game to nurture your grandkids' super sleuthing skills AND to talk about how each of them are unique. Talk about fingerprints, perhaps going online to show them pictures of the six major patterns: whorl, arch, tented arch, double loop, ulnar loop, and radial loop. Help each child determine which kind of fingerprints he or she has. Next, using an inked stamp pad and paper, take fingerprints of the family—and write their name under their set of prints. Have everyone wash and dry their hands. Next, put as many clear drinking glasses on the table as there are people playing. Have each person carefully pick up a glass, hold it for about 10 seconds without moving their fingers, and then set the glass back on the table. Help your grandkids dust the surface of each glass with a make-up brush and a little bit of baby powder. Blow off the excess powder. You should see the outlines of at least one good fingerprint. Hold a wide strip of clear tape above the clearest print and gently lower it to the surface of the glass. Carefully smooth out the tape, being careful not to smear the print. Then, life the tape and stick it onto a dark colored piece of paper. With a magnifying glass, compare each print to the ones in your super sleuth file. Can you figure out which person held which glass?

Loop

Whorl

Arch

BACKYARD MINI-GOLF

Create your very own backyard miniature golf course, using brooms or plastic baseball bats as clubs. Set cans turned on their sides (remove one or both ends to use either as a "hole" or a tunnel), plastic cups, chairs, cardboard boxes, rocks, garden gnomes…the possibilities are as endless as your imagination. If you don't have golf balls, use ping-pong balls—or tennis balls for younger children.

PAINT WITH SAND

Put sand in several small plastic containers. Add a few drops of food coloring, a different color for each container. Close the lid and shake to mix. Spread the sand on newspaper for a few minutes to let it dry, then put it back into the separate containers to make it easier to "paint" with. Using a pencil, have grandkids draw a picture on a piece of cardboard or poster board. One section at a time, help them spread a thin line of glue on the outline of the drawing. Then, sprinkle one color of sand over the glue. Shake the excess sand back into the container. Repeat for the rest of the drawing. You can also spread glue over large areas and color with sand. Allow the masterpiece to dry for about an hour before putting it on display.

HOT BERRY CIDER

A perfect warm-up for a chilly day: combine 32 oz. cranberry juice cocktail, 16 oz. apple juice, and 3 cinnamon sticks in a saucepan. Warm over low heat, stirring occasionally. Remove cinnamon sticks and serve. Serves 6.

FRIGID DIG

Looking for a cool activity on a warm day? Plan ahead. Poor water into a small plastic storage bin. Add various plastic animals and/or tub toys. Freeze until solid. On a hot day, remove the giant frozen critter cube from the storage bin and place it outside. Give your grandkids plastic kid tools, such as a hammer, garden trowel, screwdriver, or sturdy kids silverware. Let them try and chip away whatever they can to free the animals. Aid them by bringing plastic cups of warm water that they can pour over the cube to help the dig go more quickly. (If you have the time and patience, you can make the Frigid Dig more interesting by freezing it in layers. Fill the tub with water, about 1/4 full. Add a few plastic animals. Freeze. Then, add a bit of food coloring to water and pour that on top of what is already frozen. Add a few more plastic animals. After that has frozen, top it off with yet another colorful layer of water and tub toys.)

PICASSO SNOW

When winter has painted the world in white, encourage your grandkids to add a little color to the scene. Fill a small spray bottle with water, adding 10 to 12 drops of food coloring. Screw the lid back on and shake. Repeat, making a variety of colors. Then head outside. Paint faces on snowmen. Write messages in the snow. Or paint a colorful "snowbow" as an homage to Spring!

YESTERDAY & TODAY

Play a game comparing how we do things today and how they were done in the past. For example, Grandma used an encyclopedia to do research, but her grandchild uses the Internet; or Grandpa looked for library books using a card catalog while his grandchild uses a computer at the library or even at home.

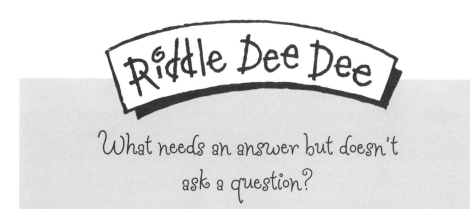

Riddle Dee Dee

What needs an answer but doesn't ask a question?

LIBRARY ADVENTURE

Take a trip to the library. Many libraries hold special family events, such as story times, arts and crafts programs, concerts, game nights, and drop-in playtime. Check to see what your local library has to offer. Or just go in and read some good books together!

BUBBLE IT UP

Make soap or bubble bath. Mix 1/2 cup mild liquid body soap, 1 tablespoon sugar or honey, and 1 egg white in a container. Pour the mixture under running water when you draw your bath. This bubble bath is great for your skin! For a foaming bubble bath, mix 1 cup almond or sunflower oil, 1/2 cup mild liquid body soap, 1/2 cup honey, and 1 tablespoon vanilla extract. Shake and pour under running water. You can also add scent to your bubble bath with a few drops of essential oils. Lavender is a favorite!

GRANDMA SPA DAY

Obviously, this isn't as relaxing as going to a REAL spa, but your grandkids will have lots of fun pampering you. Have them fix your hair, paint your nails, give you a massage, whatever you feel is appropriate for their age—and that you feel you can live with on the drive home!

FACIAL...FOR YOU AND THE KIDS!

Make your own face mask out of honey and milk. Mix 1 teaspoon of honey, 1 teaspoon of milk, and 1 teaspoon of mashed avocado. Stir with a whisk. Spread over face and leave on for 20-30 minutes. Wash off with warm water. Enjoy your soft, beautiful faces!

MEMORY TREASURE TIME CAPSULE

A lot can change in a year! Help your grandkids capture a moment in time by making a time capsule together. Have your grandkids draw a picture of their favorite memory from the past year. Ask them to tell you what was so special about that particular day or event. Write what they say on the back of the drawing and write today's date on it. Seal the drawings in a ziplock freezer storage bag. Place them in a tin, box, or plastic container. Find a place in the backyard to bury the time capsule. Take turns digging the hole and then refilling it after you've put the container in it. Together, make a map so you will remember where your Memory Treasure is buried! Set an alert on your phone for a year from now to remind you when to dig your treasure up again. You'll be surprised at how quickly a year goes by! When that day comes, have your grandchildren draw a new picture of their favorite memory from that year. Rebury all of the pictures in a new ziplock bag. This may become a favorite family tradition, which you could celebrate with fanfare and tasty treats!

KALEIDOSCOPE COOKIES

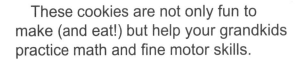

These cookies are not only fun to make (and eat!) but help your grandkids practice math and fine motor skills.

You'll Need:
Sugar cookie dough & Food coloring

For these edible works of art, use your own favorite sugar cookie recipe or a pre-packaged roll of refrigerated cookie dough. (If using refrigerated dough, allow it to soften to about room temperature.) Have Grandma preheat the oven. Divide the dough into four equal pieces and put each piece in a separate bowl. Add a few drops of food coloring to each bowl. Mix with a fork, until the color is spread evenly throughout the dough.

Take a small piece of dough (about 1 inch in diameter) and roll it into a ball. (If the dough is too soft to work with, put it in the refrigerator for 10 to 15 minutes before continuing.) Divide up the rest of the dough, rolling each piece into a ball. Next, take one ball of each color. Set them next to each other to form a diamond shape. (You can do this on a clean countertop or on a piece of wax paper.) Then, squish them together and roll them on the counter to form a cookie dough "snake," about 8 to 10 inches long. On the cookie sheet, tightly roll each "snake" into a spiral. Grandma will bake your colorful creations according to the directions on your recipe.

A SPECIAL LETTER

Join up with the kids to write a letter to a relative or friend. Have the kids decribe what they are doing or an interesting event or experience they've had. Have them draw pictures in the margins to make your letter even more appealing. Decorate the envelope too!

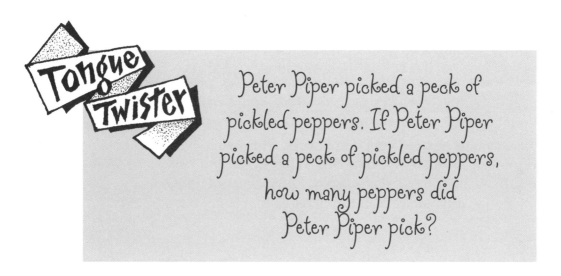

Peter Piper picked a peck of pickled peppers. If Peter Piper picked a peck of pickled peppers, how many peppers did Peter Piper pick?

IN THE FUNNY PAPERS

Draw a comic strip starring you and your grandkids. Use big sheets of newsprint or poster board from a craft store. Make up funny characters and situations or adventures.

WATCH HAIRY HARRY GROW!

   Nature never ceases to fascinate kids and grown-ups alike. Here's a project you can grow together. Take a clean nylon stocking and cut it four inches above the toe. Spoon 2 Tbsp. of grass seed into the stocking. Top it off with about 6 Tbsp. of potting soil. You should have a ball of soil about 2 inches in diameter. Tie a knot in the cut end of the stocking, so the soil will hold its round shape. Do NOT cut off the tail of the end you've tied. Tail end down, glue a set of jiggly plastic eyes on Harry. Using waterproof markers, draw a nose and mouth. Then, pour 1 to 2 inches of water into the bottom of a clean, plastic individual serving yogurt container. Place Hairy into the container, making sure the nylon tail sits in the water and Harry's head peeks above the top of the container. Refill the water daily. As the grass grows, you can help your grandkids trim Harry's green "hair."

Riddle Dee Dee

What time is it when an elephant sits on your fence?

STORY PETS

Whether your grandkids have pets or not, have them pretend they ARE their pet—or a pet they wish they had. Have them come up with stories about what their pet is thinking and what it would say if it could talk. If you're really feeling in a creative mood, try and come up with a lunch or snack idea that looks like something their pet would eat.

PHOTO SCAVENGER HUNT

Walk around your neighborhood and take a picture of something that begins with every letter of the alphabet. Or choose a letter and take pictures of objects that begin with that letter. Assemble your photos into a book.

MEET THE NEIGHBORS

Learn about your neighborhood. Ask your local police or fire station if they give tours. Or ask a local bank, store, or post office.

CELEBRATE THEIR CREATIONS!

Have your very own talent show. Hang a line of string across a room. Then use clothespins to hang all the drawings, collages, poetry, and other projects your grandchildren have been working on. Invite the family to come to a special artist's reception. Serve punch and cookies and encourage everyone to give positive critiques of the creative works. Point out something specific you like about each piece, such as the mixture of colors or the rhythm of a poem or song.

INVISIBLE INK MAGIC

Write and decipher messages in invisible ink. Make your ink by mixing water and lemon juice in a bowl. Dip a cotton swab into the mixture and write a message on a sheet of white paper. Wait for the mixture to dry. Then reveal the message by holding the paper over a warm light bulb. The heat will make the ink appear like magic!

INVENTION CENTRAL

Create a fun or unusual product. Make up an advertisement for it. Record your advertisement on video, or create a magazine or Internet ad to promote it.

CREATE A FAMILY TREE

You can make your own or find templates on the Internet. Illustrate the tree with photos or drawings.

What is the tallest building in town?

THE QUESTION BOX

Make a question box. Write questions on pieces of paper, such as "Who was your best friend?" "What was the scariest thing that ever happened to you?" "What is your favorite food?" etc. Place the papers in a box and take turns choosing and answering the questions.

WHERE'S THE TREASURE?

Hide a treasure somewhere in your house or yard. Give your grandchild clues to find it.

JEWELRY BOX TREASURES

Look through your jewelry box. Tell the story behind each piece of jewelry—who gave it to you, where did you get it, when did you wear it, etc. Let your grandchild try on special pieces as you share memories.

Tongue Twister

Toy boat. Toy boat. Toy boat.
(Who can say it the most times?)

BLAST FROM THE PAST

Look at baby books of the child, their parents or grandparents. Make a game—Who wore the funniest outfit? Who had the strangest hairstyle? Which photo was taken in an unusual location?

BE A BIRD WATCHER

Go on a bird watching hike. Keep a journal to list how many and what kinds of birds you see. Be sure to take photos or make a drawing!

HERE BIRDIE BIRDIE

Spring is an especially great time to start bird watching because the birds are pairing up and building their nests. Get a book on local birds in your area. Many park services offices have information, too.

PAPER CRANE PLAY

Remember making origami animals? They're just as much fun to make today as they were way back when. Check out an origami book from the library or purchase a book of instructions (that often includes authentic origami paper). Master making creative creatures together.

HAPPY HULA DANCE-OFF

When inclement weather strikes, take your grandkids on a trip to the islands! Help prepare them for this activity by watching videos of Polynesian or Hawaiian dancers together on the internet. This will not only inspire some awesome dance move but demonstrate that both boys and girls can play this game.

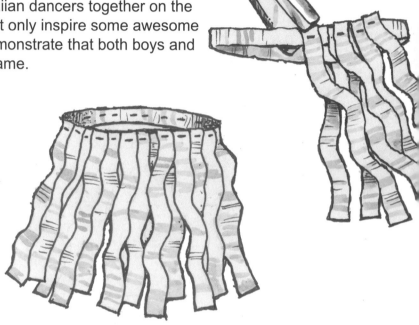

You'll need:
Crepe paper, various colors & a stapler

Cut a piece of crepe paper a few inches larger than your grandchildren's waists. Then, cut at least 15 strips of crepe paper per skirt, each about 18 inches long, or longer depending on the height of your grandchildren. The strips should hang just below their knees. Staple one end of each strip along the "waistband." Then, staple the finished skirt around the child's waist. (If you'd like a skirt you can use more than once, staple crepe paper to an elastic band big enough for children to easily pull off and on over their clothing.) Don't forget to make one for yourself! Then turn on the music and dance away. Play both fast and slow music. You may even want to choreograph a hula routine your grandkids can show to their parents.

BUSY AT THE BAR-B-QUE

When cooking outside on the bar-b-que, it can be hard to keep the kids away from the grill. Here's an idea that will not only keep them busy, but also save you from having to come up with dessert. Fill a gallon-sized ziplock bag half full of ice. Add 6 Tbsp. of rock salt. Take a pint-sized plastic bag and add 1 cup of milk or half-and-half, 2 Tbsp. sugar, and 1/2 tsp. vanilla. Seal securely. Place the pint bag into the gallon bag and seal. Shake the bag for 5 to 7 minutes. Poof! You have kid-made ice cream. If you want to branch out from the usual vanilla, try adding different flavors of extract, such as peppermint or almond. Top with sprinkles or fresh fruit and enjoy!

Riddle Dee Dee

What kind of soda can't you drink?

GOOD, CLEAN FUN!

Make bath time more fun by helping your grandkids turn the tub—and themselves—into a work of art. Mix together 1/3 C mild, clear, liquid dish detergent and 1 Tbsp. cornstarch together in a bowl. Divide the mixture into equal portions in a plastic ice cube tray. Add 1 to 2 drops of food coloring to each section. Mix with a toothpick or small spoon. Have your grandkids paint the tub in whatever theme strikes their fancy. When bath time is drawing to an end, have each artist use a washcloth to erase their artwork—until next time.

ROAD TRIP BOX

Do your kids, and grandkids, a favor by making a Bon Voyage Box to give to each grandchild before they head out on a family vacation. Individually wrap small treats inside, such as fish crackers, a small notepad and stickers, plastic sunglasses, a coloring book and small box of crayons, etc. A "dollar" store is a great place to pick up a few inexpensive items that will keep kids busy on the road. Don't forget to include a self-addressed, stamped postcard with your address on it so the kids can keep in touch with you while they are away.

SAIL AWAY SNACKS

Add a little fun and fancy to snack time by turning an apple into a boat. Combine 1/4 cup peanut butter, 3 Tbsp. chopped peanuts, 1/4 cup crispy rice cereal, and 3 Tbsp raisins. Cut an apple in half and scoop out the core, leaving extra room for the peanut butter mixture. Spoon the mixture into the apple halves. Make sails by cutting 2 slices of cheese into triangles and sticking them upright into the peanut mixture. Two apple boats (containing three of the four food groups!), ready to set sail!

FUN FOOD SURPRISE

Blindfold each other and try to guess different flavors of jellybeans by taste alone. Try this game with other candies, cookies, or foods.

I SEE STARS!

Bring the night sky indoors! On a piece of dark blue paper, draw your grandchild's favorite constellation—marking the placement of every star with an X. Poke a fairly large hole in the middle of each X with a safety pin. Head to a darkened room, hold a flashlight behind the paper, and voilà—instant stars!

CIRCLE THE WAGONS

For a wild West themed snack, have your grandkids put frosting on 1/4 of a graham cracker, then top with another 1/4 of graham cracker. Spread a bit of frosting on the top graham cracker—and place two large marshmallows, flat sides together, on top. Attach four circular hard candy "wheels" to the wagon bed with a bit more frosting. For a finishing touch, put a dab of frosting between two animal crackers to hold them together, so they will stand up. Set the animals in front of the wagon and you're ready to point your pioneer wagon west— or simply eat it!

FROSTY SAILING SHIPS

Fill an ice cube tray with water. Put in the freezer until partially frozen. Put an open paper cocktail umbrella in the middle of each ice cube. Allow to freeze solid. Fashion an aluminum foil "river" in the backyard with the garden hose running slowly on one end. Sail the ships down the river, seeing which ship makes it to the end first.

CREATE A TOTEM POLE

Totem poles are an important part of some Native American cultures. They are used to represent families or tribes. You can make your own totem pole by gluing construction paper over a paper towel tube. Use a pencil to divide the tube into three or four sections. Decorate each section with a different animal that is special to you. Traditional totem pole animals include bears, beavers, seals, and fish, but you can choose any animals you like.

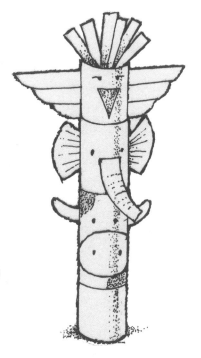

STICK IT WALL MURAL

Give each child a small pad of sticky notes and crayons or washable markers. Have them draw portraits of friends and family, different animals, imaginary creatures, or whatever their hearts desire. Then, have them create their own art gallery by sticking them on the wall. Easy on, easy off!

Riddle Dee Dee

Which is faster, heat or cold?

SHOEBOX DOLLHOUSE

Open an empty shoebox. Cover with construction paper or paint with markers or craft paint and let dry. Lay the box on its side. Make furniture from small pieces of cardboard. For example, fold a piece of cardboard to make a chair, or cut down a toilet paper tube and lay a small square of cardboard on top to make a table. Cut pictures out of magazines to create furniture or artwork. You can stack another shoebox on top to make a second floor if desired.

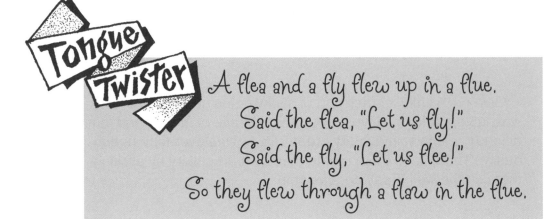
MAKE PLANS AND START A GARDEN

Let your grandkids actually help you plan what kind of garden you want to have. Will it be a flower garden or a vegetable garden or some of both?
Should you grow some things from seeds?
(More magical!) Or buy some already-sprouted plants and transfer them to your garden?
(More immediately gratifying!)

P.S. Homegrown tomatoes are hard to beat!

PRETTY PLACEMATS

Make placemats using poster board, markers, or paint. You can even get them laminated at an office supply store or mail center.

GARDEN IN A BOTTLE

You will need:

- A large glass container, such as a fishbowl, a jar, or a wide-mouthed vase
- Cacti or other succulent plants
- Potting soil
- Pebbles
- White sand
- A spoon

1. Fill the container with 1 1/2 inches of pebbles.

2. Add about 2 1/2 inches of potting soil.

3. Use the spoon to make a small hole in the soil. Insert one of the cacti. Spread the dirt over the roots to cover them completely.

4. Add the other plants, arranging them as you like.

5. Add 1/4 inch of white sand around the plants.

6. Place your terrarium in the sun. Add a little bit of water every two weeks or so.

To create a fairy garden, add colorful rocks, small mushroom figurines, and other details to your terrarium.

SWEET HARVEST CORN COBS

The next time you're making marshmallow rice cereal treats, why not fashion them into calico corn cobs? Cut up several brown paper bags into long strips. Crumple the strips to look like the top of a corn husk. Set aside. Grease or butter a large piece of waxed paper to use as your work surface. Prepare your favorite rice cereal treats. With buttered fingers, have grandchildren roll about 1/2 cup of the mixture into corn cob shapes. Decorate each cob with mini rainbow-colored baking chips. Insert a few pieces of paper bag husk into the top of the cob for decoration. Be sure to remove before eating!

Riddle Dee Dee

What bone has a sense of humor?

BUTTER THEM UP

Preparing holidays meals is easier when the grandkids are happily occupied. Here's a way that grandkids can help with the meal, while burning off a little energy at the same time. Pour 1/2 pint of heavy whipping cream into a pint jar, then seal it tight. Have the grandkids take turns shaking the jar, until a ball of butter forms inside. Add a dash of salt, and yellow food coloring, if desired. Using a spoon, mix well, and press out any excess liquid. Add a spoonful of honey for a special homemade treat.

GO FISH

Although this fishing hole won't supply any fish for dinner, it will provide lots of indoor fun on a rainy day. Cut out simple fish shapes from construction paper. If you want to get fancy, you can cut out other critters, as well, such as alligators, frogs, and dolphins. Decorate as desired! Stick a paper clip through the paper near where the critter's mouth would be. Bend the paper clip up, so that it's easier to "catch." Tie a piece of yarn or string (about 6 inches long for toddlers, up to 2 feet for older children) to a ruler, wooden spoon, or chopstick. (For younger children, you can simply have them hold the string and forego the pole!) Attach a paper clip to the bottom on the yarn, bending the open end to make a hook. Use a small blanket as your pond— or draw one on paper. Put your critters into the pond and go fish!

Riddle Dee Dee

What has four wheels and flies?

FRUIT & VEGETABLE STAMPS

Make stamps out of fruits and vegetables and decorate some paper. Cut up or slice "hard" fruits and vegetables, such as apples, potatoes, and carrots. Use craft paint or a stamp pad to ink the stamps. Press them onto sheets or paper. How many different colors and shapes can you make? Can you combine shapes to make a pattern or picture?

MAKE YOUR OWN WRAPPING PAPER

Decorate rolls of craft paper or plain white wrapping paper. Use markers, rubber stamps (or your fruit and veggie stamps), craft paint, stickers, etc. Use the paper to wrap a special gift for a family member of friend.

SWEET VEGETABLE TREATS

If it's tough getting your grandkids to eat their vegetables, here are two desserts that sneak them into the recipe in a delicious way.

Zucchini Brownies: Put one egg, slightly beaten, into a measuring cup. Then add enough milk to make 2/3 cup liquid. Put 1/3 cup oil, 1 1/2 cup sugar, 2 tsp. vanilla, 2 cups flour (you can use part whole wheat, if desired), 1 tsp. salt, 1 1/2 tsp baking soda, 1/2 cup cocoa, and 2 cups grated zucchini into a mixing bowl. Add egg mixture. Mix thoroughly and pour into a 9" x 13" pan. Bake at 350° for 30 to 35 minutes.

Crazy Tomato Cake: Sift 2 cups of flour. Add 1/2 tsp salt, 1 tsp. cinnamon, 1/2 tsp each nutmeg and ground cloves, and 1/2 tsp baking soda. Resift mixture. Cream 2 Tbsp. butter and 1 cup sugar in a large bowl. Adding a little at a time, stir flour mixture into butter mixture, along with 1 can of condensed tomato soup (10 1/2 oz). Fold in 1 cup chopped walnuts and 1 cup raisins. Pour into a 9" x 13" pan and bake at 350° for about 45 minutes. Make this at home and then have your grandkids guess your secret ingredient!

Carrot Raisin Bran Cookies
Beat together 1 cup firmly packed brown sugar and 1 cup softened butter until fluffy. Add 1 cup (2 medium) shredded carrots, 1 tsp. vanilla, and 1 egg. Blend well. Add 1 1/2 cup flour, 1 tsp. cinnamon, and 1/2 tsp. baking soda. Mix well. Stir in 2 1/2 cups bran flakes cereal with raisins. Drop by teaspoons on ungreased cookie sheet. Bake at 375° for 9 to 14 minutes. Cool 1 minute before removing from cookie sheet. Makes 5 1/2 dozen cookies.

A skunk sat on a stump and thunk the stump stunk, but the stump thunk the skunk stunk.

HAMBURGER COOKIES

While the grown-ups are cooking burgers on the grill, have the grandkids help you make these easy-to-assemble burger cookies for dessert. Spread 1/2 tsp. of frosting on the flat side of a vanilla wafer cookie. Place 2 Tbsp. of shredded coconut and a couple drops of green food coloring in a jar, close and shake. Place a little of the dyed coconut on the frosting for "lettuce." Top with one chocolate-covered mint patty candy or one chocolate-covered mint cookie. Put 1/2 tsp. of frosting on the flat side of another vanilla wafer cookie and use it as the top "bun." Brush the top of the "burger" with a small amount of honey and sprinkle it with sesame seeds. Make one "burger" for each person at the bar-b-que.

BOREDOM BUSTERS

Write activity ideas on slips of paper. Ideas could include "Play 20 Questions," "Act out a favorite story," "Read a book," "Watch a favorite movie," "Go for a walk around the block," and "Make a card and send it to a friend." Next time your grandchildren are bored, reach into the bag and choose an activity to share!

MAGIC MARSHMALLOW PUFFS

Here's a snack and a magic trick, all rolled into one! Open a package of roll and bake crescent-shaped dinner rolls. Divide the rolls into individual triangles. Combine 1/4 cup sugar and 1 tsp. cinnamon in a small bowl. Melt 1/4 cup of butter. Dip large marshmallows into melted butter and then roll in cinnamon sugar mixture. Wrap a dough triangle around the marshmallow, completely covering it, and squeeze the edges tight. Dip filled roll in melted butter and place the roll, butter side down, in a muffin tin. Place muffin pan on a cookie sheet or sheet of foil in a pre-heated oven at 375° for 10 to 15 minutes, until golden brown. If desired, make glaze by mixing 1/2 cup powdered sugar, 2 to 3 tsp. of milk, and 1/2 tsp. vanilla in a small bowl. Drizzle glaze over slightly cooled puffs. When your grandkids bite into their sweet treat, ask them where the disappearing marshmallow went!

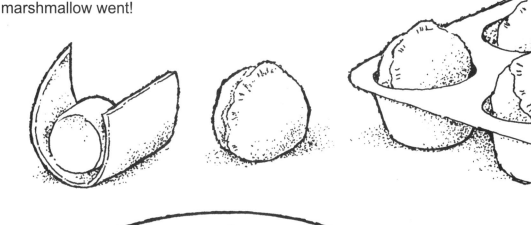

Why did the cowboy buy a dachshund?

SET SAIL IN A BOTTLE

Make and sail water-bottle boats.

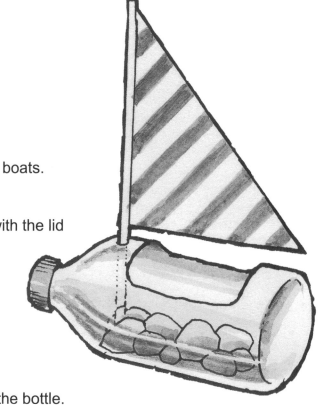

You will need:
- An empty water bottle with the lid
- A straw
- A piece of paper
- Small stones or gravel
- Markers
- Scissors
- Tape
- A screwdriver

1. Remove the label from the bottle.

2. Have an adult cut a rectangle out of the side of the bottle.

3. Create a mast by decorating the paper with markers to make a sail. Tape the paper to the straw.

4. Have an adult use the screwdriver to punch a hole near the top of the bottle to hold the mast. Slide the mast into the hole.

5. Fill the bottle with stones to give it weight.

6. Take your boat to a local pond or sail it in the bathtub or kitchen sink.

BRING SPRINGTIME INSIDE

When winter seems to go on forever, help your grandkids anticipate the coming of spring by planting flower bulbs indoors. Tulips and daffodils are great choices and bloom in about 4 to 6 weeks. Put flower bulbs in a bowl of pebbles and water. Be sure to keep the base of the bulb wet at all times. Put the bowl in a dark place for about 10 days, until the roots have formed. Then, move to a sunny windowsill and watch for the first sign of spring to appear!

SEARCHING FOR SPRINGTIME

When winter is on its way out, take your grandkids for a walk to look for signs of spring. Give them each a small card with a list (or use stickers with pictures, if they are too young to read) of things you are looking for, such as a bird, a flower, a leaf, a bicycle, a cloud, the sun, a worm, etc. Repeat this each week along the same route, taking note of how things are changing as spring is getting closer.

Riddle Dee Dee

What kind of fish chases a mouse?

LIGHT UP A LAVA LAMP

You will need:

- An empty water bottle
- Cooking oil
- Water
- An antacid tablet
- Food coloring

1. Fill the bottle 2/3 of the way with oil and the rest of the way with water. Leave about an inch of space at the top.

2. Add a few drops of food coloring.

3. Break the antacid tablet into 3 or 4 pieces and add to the water. As the tablet dissolves, the water will start to fizz.

4. You can create more bubbles by adding more antacid tablets.

Riddle Dee Dee

What has four legs, but can't walk?

COOL IDEA FOR A HOT DAY

When the temperatures soar, saturate a large, clean sponge with water and send the grandkids outside to play a wet and wild game of catch.

CRAZY CAKE QUILT

Here's a twist on traditional cupcakes that's fun for grandkids to decorate. Have Grandma bake a 9" x 13" sheet cake. Let cool. Cut it into 24 squares. Have grandkids use tubes of frosting, sprinkles, and other festive candy decorations to top each piece with a different design. Then, put the cake back together to form a quilt-inspired treat.

NEIGHBORHOOD BINGO

Play Neighborhood Bingo. Cut out pictures of local landmarks or places and glue them to pieces of cardboard. Take a walk or a ride and see who can fill up their Bingo card first. Rainy day? Play this game indoors using household objects.

KID-SIZED CAR WASH

Need a way to clean toys after lots of dirty, sticky play? One way is to put any plastic, washable toys into a mesh laundry bag and attach the bag to the top rack of the dishwasher. However, you can also turn clean-up time into fun time. Outside, fill a large plastic tub with soapy water. Give your grandkids each an old toothbrush. Throw all of their washable toys in the tub and then take them out, one at a time, to give them a good, soapy scrub. Have them set the clean toys inside a plastic grocery bag. When they are finished, give everything in the bag a good rinse and let them dry. Then, you're ready for play time all over again!

TEA TIME!

A tea party is a treat for both boys and girls, young and old. Yes, you can have it at the kitchen table, but also consider holding one on a blanket in front of the fire, on a picnic table at the park, in a grand-kid's pop-up play tent, or a backyard playhouse. Here are a few ideas to help inspire you further:

• Have everyone refer to each other as Ma'am and Sir. Encourage good manners!

• Put 1/2 tsp jam in the bottom of each teacup to sweeten traditional tea—or combine lemonade and sweet tea.

• Serve finger sandwiches cut with cookie cutters. Try raisin bread with apple butter or cucumber and cream cheese with fresh mint leaves.

• Have a contest to see who can stack sugar cubes the highest!

• Play Tea Bag games, such as Tea Bag Toss (toss unused teabags into the top of a teapot) or Tic-Tac-Tea (make a Tic-Tac-Toe grid on the floor with masking tape and have grandkids try and toss tea bags into three adjoining squares).

• Have grandkids make their own British fascinators to wear during the party. Attach curled ribbons, tulle, shapes cut from crepe paper, and plastic flowers to a hairband. Feel free to go big!

OPEN FOR BUSINESS

You can set up a "store" right in your home! Let children arrange household objects, such as shoes, books, jewelry, or kitchen utensils, in a display and open their own store. Take turns being the salesperson and the customer. Kids can make signs to advertise prices and special sales. Use play money or real coins to help them practice math skills, such as addition, subtraction, and multiplication.

BRING IT TO ME!

This is a great game to play when you need a little time to rest, but the grandkids are still filled with energy. Place a blanket or plastic tablecloth on the floor. Then, give the grandkids directions, such as "Bring me something round!" or "Bring me something blue!" Continue until you've caught your breath. Then, have them put everything away by telling them to "Put away something round!" etc.

ACROSS THE MILES

Thanks to modern technology, keeping in touch with grandkids who live in a different city, state, or even country, isn't difficult. It just takes a little time and thought. Here are a few ideas to get your creative juices flowing:

✳ Purchase postcards that showcase your state. Send one to your grandkids every few weeks.

✳ Put your own address (and a stamp!) on postcards and send them to your grandchildren, to encourage them to write to you.

✳ Have set times to video chat every month. Make sure it's when the kids are awake and fed! You may even want to play a game of I Spy while you're chatting, making sure that what you spy is visible through the video camera.

✳ Text pictures or videos of yourself doing something fun to the grandkids on a regular basis.

✳ Start a book club. Send the grandkids a book and then video chat to discuss it.

✳ If you can't be there for a birthday, send a card for every year your grandchild is celebrating, e.g., if she's six years old, send her six cards!

✳ Celebrate a grandchild's 1/2 year birthday, since a whole year is a long time in a child's life!

✳ Send your grandkids' disposable cameras and ask them to take photos of what they're doing. Include a postage-paid envelope, so it's easy for them to return the camera to you. Develop the photos and enjoy a window into your grandkids' everyday lives.

✳ Take advantage of a grandchild's interest in technology by emailing back and forth and/or posting messages to each other on social media.

✳ Keep a calendar that lists the activities your grandkids are doing, so you will remember to ask them how these events went. You may also want to keep a list of the names of your grandchildren's friends, so you can ask how they are by name the next time you chat.

✳ Send your grandchild a digital photo frame to use as a nightlight. Fill it with photos of things you've done together.

✳ Record a story (whether it's an original tale or simply a book you read aloud) on one of the online bedtime story sites that allows it to be downloaded onto a child's own electronic device.

✳ Send a "goodie" box once a month. Keep it simple and inexpensive. Tie goodies into any holidays that occur that month. Include knick-knacks such as coloring books, a fun pen or pencil, comic books, window clings, socks, temporary tattoos, stickers, book marks, fun shoelaces, a shell picked up on a recent vacation, or toys from a dollar store.

✳ When Christmas comes around, have YOUR photo taken with Santa and send it along to the grandkids.

ALL IN THE FAMILY

Have a family photo made into a simple jigsaw puzzle with a limited number of pieces. (This option is available through many of the photo album sites online.) Puzzles not only make a fun family activity, but also help with eye-hand coordination, problem solving, fine motor skills, and color recognition.

HONOR OUR VETERANS!

Spend some time talking about the bravery of the veterans who fought in our country's wars. Through the VFW or American Legion, find a veteran to visit together. The grandkids can bring cards or thank-you notes. Help compile a list of questions to help the grandkids learn about the veteran's experiences in the service of the U.S.A.

Riddle Dee Dee

Can giraffes have babies?

CLEAN UP GAMES

Let's be honest—it's tough to stop playing long enough to clean up. Here are a few ideas to help make chores feel less like work and more like play.

- Put items away by color.

- Put items away by category. For instance, "First, let's pick up everything round!"

- To get ready for bedtime, put toys to sleep, too.

- Clean out the dishwasher by giving everyone a different item (e.g., spoons, plastic cups, plates, etc.) they are responsible to either take out of the dishwasher and stack on the counter (if they are small) or put away (if they are tall enough to reach the proper cabinet.)

- Set a timer and see if you can beat last time's record for tidying up.

- Similar to musical chairs: pick up toys while the music's playing; freeze when it stops!

- Give grandkids an oven mitt to use to pick things up. It takes a bit longer, but it's more fun!

- Using a marker, draw a face on a gym sock. Let grandkids use the Dust Bunny to help you dust.

- Put masking tape in a square on the kitchen floor. Have grandkids use a small broom or brush to sweep everything into the square. Then, you can sweep what's in the square into a dustpan.

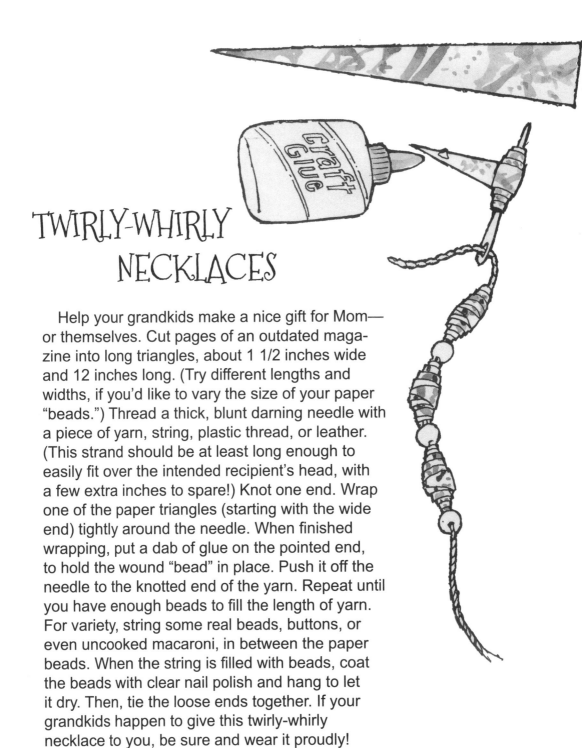

TWIRLY-WHIRLY NECKLACES

Help your grandkids make a nice gift for Mom—or themselves. Cut pages of an outdated magazine into long triangles, about 1 1/2 inches wide and 12 inches long. (Try different lengths and widths, if you'd like to vary the size of your paper "beads.") Thread a thick, blunt darning needle with a piece of yarn, string, plastic thread, or leather. (This strand should be at least long enough to easily fit over the intended recipient's head, with a few extra inches to spare!) Knot one end. Wrap one of the paper triangles (starting with the wide end) tightly around the needle. When finished wrapping, put a dab of glue on the pointed end, to hold the wound "bead" in place. Push it off the needle to the knotted end of the yarn. Repeat until you have enough beads to fill the length of yarn. For variety, string some real beads, buttons, or even uncooked macaroni, in between the paper beads. When the string is filled with beads, coat the beads with clear nail polish and hang to let it dry. Then, tie the loose ends together. If your grandkids happen to give this twirly-whirly necklace to you, be sure and wear it proudly!

SELF-PORTRAITS

Purchase large craft paper sheets, or tape sheets of drawing paper together to make a sheet large enough to fit your grandchild! Have your grandchild lie on the paper and carefully trace around his or her body. Have grandchildren finish their self-portrait by drawing in their face, hair, fingernails, etc. Have a mirror nearby, so they can look at themselves as they work. Either draw on clothing or glue on cloth remnants. When complete, cut out each portrait and tack it to the wall. Talk about how your grandchildren look alike, and how they are different, from each other.

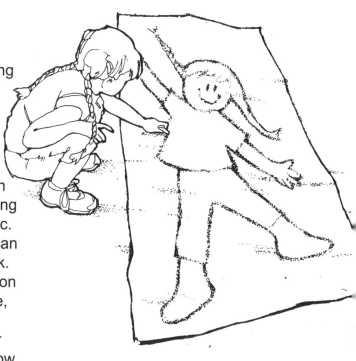

Shy Shelly says
she shall sew sheets.

HOMEMADE SNOW GLOBES

   Make it snow any month of the year, even if you live in Florida! Give each grandchild the lid from a small, clean glass jar. Glue tiny plastic animals, the tips of plastic greenery (to make minia- ture Christmas trees), or any other small, decorative items to the inside of the lid. Let dry overnight. Fill the jar with baby oil or corn syrup, adding a few Tbsp. of water to reach desired consistency. Add glitter, sparkles, or metallic confetti to make snow. Put glue around the inside of the decorated lid and seal the jar shut. Let dry for several hours. Then shake the jar upside down so the animal scene is on the bottom, and let the blizzard begin!

PAINT A ROCK

   Find a small flat smooth rock and let the shape inspire your grandchild's image or message. They can use permanent markers or acrylic paint to design. Place these fun rocks in your own garden, or hide them in other spaces to surprise and delight those who discover them!

POETRY SLAM

Learn about different types of poems, such as haiku, concrete poems, cinquains, or limericks. You can find information at the library or on the Internet. Then choose a style and write some poems of your own. Print them and make a poetry book.

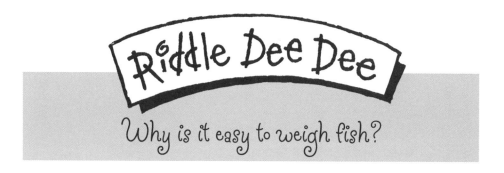

Riddle Dee Dee

Why is it easy to weigh fish?

RATTLE UP A RAIN STICK

Rain sticks are traditional instruments made of hollow cactus branches filled with thorns and pebbles. Ancient cultures used them to call rain spirits. You can make your own using a long cardboard container with a lid (such as a potato-chip container). Fill the tube with pebbles, rice, buttons, plastic beads, etc.—any small object that will rattle and make noise! Decorate the outside by covering it with paper and painting or adding stickers. Tap on your rain stick or flip it up and down to make noise—and maybe even summon a storm!

CHALK MURALS!

Buy a pail of sidewalk chalk. (Most of it comes in pails these days; either in toy stores, hobby stores or chain drugs.) Let the kids brighten up your driveway or sidewalk with their expressive designs.

GRANDKID GARLANDS

Remember making a paper doll chain when you were a kid? Why not introduce your grandkids to the same easy-to-make activity? Fold a piece of paper (newspaper, construction paper, butcher paper, etc.) at least 12 inches long into 4 or more equal sections. Use a ruler to help keep your sections the same size. On the top section of the paper, draw a design that touches the folded edge in AT LEAST one place. Try people, trees, animals, hearts, snowflakes, etc. Carefully cut out the design, making sure you do not cut away all of the paper on the folded edge. Open up your garland. Have your grandkids decorate it with crayons, markers, glitter, puffy paints… whatever strikes your fancy. Now that they've watched you, help your grandkids create garlands of their own design.

TAKE IT APART

Most of us have something laying around that no longer works, such as an old radio, telephone, watch, calculator, or camera. Place the item on a big white sheet so nothing gets lost, and have your grandchild sit down with the item. Use a screwdriver to take the back off. Then let them take the item apart, investigate all the parts, and try to put it back together again. Or they can make art or creative sculptures out of the pieces.

(Note: Keep all small parts away from young children.)

What did the beach say when the tide came in?

GO FISH!

Tropical fish can be a lot of fun, whether it's just a simple goldfish or a small aquarium. For a very small investment and just a little time, you can be the proud owner of your own underwater world that will keep children amazed!

TAKE ME OUT TO THE BALLGAME

The great thing about baseball (or softball) is that you don't have to live in a major league city to enjoy going to a game. There are plenty of baseball and softball teams, both men and women, boys and girls. And one thing you can be sure of: where there's a game you'll always find hot dogs and peanuts.

Riddle Dee Dee

What's full of holes but still holds water?

TAKE A HIKE!

First make some custom trail mix the night before. Take turns making suggestions. Here are some thoughts to spark ideas: granola, M&M's, coconut, banana chips, chocolate chips, peanuts (check for allergies!), dried pineapple, a favorite cereal, mini marshmallows. Next morning pack a lunch and some of your trail mix in sandwich bags and head out! Look for nature trails and walking paths.

RIDDLE ANSWER: A SPONGE!

WINDY DAY DANCE CONTEST

When the wind is blowing, it's a great time to dance off a little extra energy with the grandkids. Hand out strips of crepe paper, scarves, or plastic bags—then hold on tight! Turn on the music and dance as the music, and gusts, move you!

WINDY DAY CHIMES

When the wind is ready to play, your grandkids will be, too. Prepare for the music a windy day can create by helping your grandkids make their own windchime. Poke holes around the edges of a tin foil pie plate. Thread various lengths of strings through each hole, knotting them at the top to secure them. Have children thread bells along the string, as well as any other items they think might be musical in the wind. Tying an old spoon or fork at the bottom of each string will give the chimes a little additional ballast, beauty, and musicality. To hang the windchime, poke a hole in the middle of the disposable tin foil pie plate. Thread string through the hole and knot it so it can be hung.

Riddle Dee Dee

Why does Dracula have bad manners?

CATCH SOME FIREFLIES!

Get a glass jar with a metal top and poke some holes in it. When your Grandkid catches a firefly (the best way is to bring your hand up under it and then put your other hand on top) gently put it into the jar and put the holey top back on. See how many you can catch in an hour's time. When you are done, take the lid off the jar and leave it outside so the fireflies can get back to doing whatever it is that fireflies do.

BACKYARD CAMPOUT!

Nothing is more fun that pitching a tent in your own back yard during the summer. It's safe and it's near a bathroom and a kitchen! But make it like real camping…bring a lantern and some flashlights, some books, a deck of cards, some snacks, some simple board games and you'll be roughing it with the best of 'em.

RAINBOW ETCHINGS

Show your grandchildren how to use crayons in a new way by helping them etch a work of art. Have each child color a paper plate HEAVILY with areas of different colors. Then, have them color over the entire plate with a black crayon until no other color can be seen. Open the end of a paper clip. Using the "sharp" end of the paper clip, help your grandchildren scratch a picture though only the black crayon, revealing the colors beneath. Polish the finished artwork with a paper towel or tissue.

GO FOR A WALK! BUT FIRST...

Help build some extra-added excitement into taking a walk around the block by first making your own walking sticks. Your first outing may be to find the perfect stick! Once each grandchild has acquired a stick that is just the right size, have them decorate them with markers. If your grandchildren are a little older, they can also use acrylic or enamel paint. Glue on small treasures like feathers, buttons, or sequins, if so desired. Then, keep track of how many miles you and your walking sticks can travel together over time.

Riddle Dee Dee

Why are teddy bears never hungry?

PRETZEL CABIN

Everyone loves making a gingerbread house over the holidays. Here's a variation you can easily put together with your grandkids anytime during the year! Rinse out, and dry, a small milk carton. Staple the top of the carton shut. Set the carton upright on a paper plate and spread peanut butter along one of the sides. Line up stick pretzels, horizontally, bottom to top, on top of the peanut butter. Repeat on each side, including the "roof." Your grandchildren may have to bite off the ends of the pretzels to make them fit! Play with the pretzel "pattern" to fashion a door and windows. Let the cabin harden. Decorate using tubes of colored icing, if desired.

BLOW BUBBLES!

Sit on the front steps and blow bubbles! It's great fun to try to pop them as they float and sure to inspire some giggles. In addition, you can teach your kids a great way to release things that are worrying them. Talk about things that are on their mind, then describe how to "blow a bubble; picture the thing that's bothering you in the bubble and watch it float away". Do this over and over again. The breathing process involved with blowing bubbles is proven to reduce stress!

SHOEBOX GUITAR

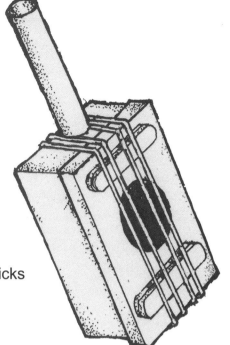

You will need:

- Shoe box
- Paper towel roll
- Four to six rubber bands
- Paint
- Craft glue or hot glue gun and glue sticks
- Paintbrush
- Scissors
- Drinking glass or mug

1. Paint the shoebox and the lid whatever color you want the guitar to be. You can also paint the paper towel roll and craft sticks if you like. Let the paint dry.
2. Using the glass or mug, cut a circle in the center of the box lid. This will be your sound hole. Put the lid on the box. Glue four craft sticks, one on top of the other, between the hole and the short side of the box so they are parallel to the short side of the shoe box.
3. Cut a hole in the side of the box. Slide the paper towel roll into the hole. This is the neck of your guitar.
4. Stretch four to six rubber bands around the box the long way, so they lay over the hole.
5. To play your shoebox guitar, pluck or strum the rubber bands. Make sure your rubber bands are large enough to stretch around the box without stretching too much so the bands don't snap.

For more musical fun, make a drum out of a canister. You can use the plastic lid that comes on many canisters, such as a coffee can or breadcrumb can. Start your own band!

INSTA-BAND

There's nothing like making music together to add a little fun to a quiet afternoon. Here are a few instruments you can make with little muss and fuss:

TAMBOURINE—Put dried beans into a disposable foil pie pan. Staple a second pie pan on top and shake. You can also use paper plates for a softer sound. For a less "authentic" tambourine, carefully put dried beans into a clean, empty soda can and cover the hole with a piece of duct tape.

DRUM—Almost anything can become a drum… plastic containers (any size, empty or full), books, cardboard boxes, empty soda cans, metal mixing bowls turned upside-down. You name it! Add chopsticks, or paper towel tubes, for drumsticks and your percussion section is ready to go!

MARACAS—Fill plastic Easter eggs with dried beans, pennies, or small candies. If you want a more authentic look, put the egg between two plastic spoons and then wrap white first-aid tape around the egg and spoons to make a handle. Decorate the tape with markers for a more performance-worthy instrument!

HARMONICA— Take 2 wide popsicle sticks and cut a piece of paper about the same size. Put the paper between the popsicle sticks. Tightly wrap a rubber band around one end of the popsicle sticks. Break a wooden toothpick in half. Slide one half of the toothpick between the popsicle sticks, under the paper, inside, next to the rubber band. Put the other half toothpick between the popsicle sticks on the opposite end—above the paper. Wrap that end tightly with another rubber band. Hold the "harmonica" up to your mouth and blow air in and out between the sticks.

PAN FLUTE—Cut plastic straws into 4 different lengths, with two pieces of each length. Put each matching pair together. Arrange them flat on the table from the shortest to the longest, all even on the bottom end. Secure them together with tape. Blow along the even end to get the tunes started.

CHINESE GONG—Decorate a disposable foil roasting pan with stickers. Wrap electrical tape around an unsharpened pencil, dowel, or chopstick to form a ball. Hold the pan with one hand, letting it dangle in front of you, and strike it with the electrical tape wrapped "hammer" for a different take on a cymbals-like sound.

KAZOO—Cover one end of a cardboard paper towel or toilet paper tube with a square of wax paper. Secure it with a rubber band. Now the grandparent (not the kids!) can poke a hole (you can poke several, if you're using a paper towel tube) with something small and pointy, such as the sharp end of a cake tester or candy thermometer. Hum or repeat the word "do" into the open end. A less attractive, but equally musical, kazoo can be made by simply folding a piece of waxed paper over a comb. Put it against your lips and hum!

CLUCK CUP—Instead of a cow bell, why not add a Cluck Cup to your band? Poke a hole in the bottom of a plastic cup. Thread one end of 18 to 20 inches of cotton string through the hole. Secure the string on the outside of the bottom of the cup by wrapping it around a paper clip. Cut about 1/3 of a single paper towel and dampen it with water. Fold the piece of towel into a small square and then pull the square down the string that is hanging from the inside of the cup, in short bursts. It will sound like a chicken clucking!

CYMBALS—Never underestimate the appeal of two pan lids for an impromptu pair of cymbals!

Once your band is assembled, try to play a song that everyone knows, such as "Twinkle, Twinkle Little Star." Schedule a special performance for Mom and Dad—or become a marching band and take a musical tour of the neighborhood.

PINT-SIZED VOLCANO

Here's an outdoor science experiment that's fast and fun. Take two small paper cups. Fill the bottom of one with 1/4 cup baking soda. Set it on a flat surface on a paper plate. Place 4 to 6 drops of red food coloring on top of the baking soda. Poke a hole, about the size of a dime, in the bottom of the second cup. Place the second cup upside-down on top of the first paper cup to make a "mountain." Pour 1/4 cup of vinegar into the hole until the volcano begins to erupt. The more vinegar you pour in, the more "volcanic foam" will flow out. If you want a little extra sparkle, you can add 1 tsp. of glitter to the baking soda.

Riddle Dee Dee

Where is the ocean the deepest?

APPLE PIE SMOOTHIES

This quick snack is reminiscent of apple pie à la mode—in a glass! Put 8 oz. of applesauce, 1/4 tsp. cinnamon, 1 cup frozen vanilla yogurt, and 3/4 cup milk into a blender and process until smooth. Pour into glasses. Serve with straw and spoons. Serves 2–3.

SAILING STRAWS

Outside, fill a plastic storage container with water to about the halfway point. Float several bath toys in it. Your grandkids can have races, trying to move the toys across the tub by blowing them with their straws. They can also simply blow bubbles into the tub.

ROUND ABOUT RAINBOWS

Finding fun, creative ways to help small grandchildren improve their fine motor skills is a gift any grandparent can give over and over again. Here's one easy way that transforms itself into a colorful work of art. First, draw a simple shape on a piece of paper, such as the outline of a person, tree, house, or even an abstract squiggle. Have your grandchild trace around the outside of the shape you've drawn, as close to your lines as he or she can. Repeat going around the outside of each preceding line in another color until the entire page is filled. Hang on the wall with a pride-filled smile!

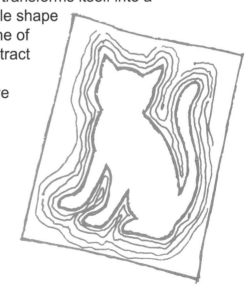

RAINBOW SNACK STACKS

Here's a colorful treat everyone will love to eat! Make your favorite sugar cookie dough recipe or purchase refrigerated pre-made dough at the store. If using the latter, allow it to warm to room temperature. Divide the dough into at least 4 equal parts, putting each portion into a glass bowl. Add a few drops of food coloring to each portion to make different colors of the rainbow. Thoroughly mix the different colors of food coloring into the divided dough with a fork. On a sheet of waxed paper, pat each color of dough into a rectangular strip about 4 inches wide and 1/4 inch thick.

Stack the different colored dough rectangles one on top of the another. Press gently to help them stick to each other. Wrap the rainbow dough in waxed paper and refrigerate overnight, or for at least one hour. When you're ready to bake, preheat the oven to the temperature stated in the recipe. Cut the layered dough into 1/4 inch slices. Gently curve each slice into an arched rainbow shape. Put the rainbows on a cookie sheet and have Grandma bake according to directions.

Tongue Twister

Friendly Frank flips fine flapjacks.

HIDDEN IMAGES

Here's a new way your grandchildren can paint with watercolors. Put a piece of wax paper over a piece of drawing paper. Draw a picture, or write a message, with a pencil on the waxed paper. Press hard! Remove the waxed paper and brush a very fine "wash" of watercolor paint over the top of the drawing paper. Watch your hidden image magically appear!

HOLE-IN-ONE MAGIC TRICK

Here's a fun way to help your grandkids see how their brain and eyes can play a magic trick on each other. Have them look through an empty cardboard toilet paper tube with one eye. Keeping both eyes open, have them run their free hand slowly along the side of the tube from its farthest point all the way up to their nose. At one point, they'll see a hole in their hand! Explain how their brain is putting the different things that each eye sees together to form one picture.

Riddle Dee Dee

Why do birds fly south in the winter?

Riddle Dee Dee

What did one toilet say to the other toilet?

IMPROMPTU PUPPET SHOW

You don't need store-bought puppets to put on a great show! Decorate brown paper bags, using the bottom flap as the mouth. Use paper plates attached to a popsicle stick. Dress up fruits and vegetables, such as a carrot, stalk of celery, potato, apple, or banana. Use socks or mittens that no longer have a mate. Use Styrofoam balls, with a hole cut in the bottom for your finger. After you've helped your grandkids get their cast of puppets together, encourage them to act out a scene from one of their favorite movies or bedtime stories—or see if they'd like to make up a story of their own. If you happen to be babysitting, video a performance to text to Mom and Dad via phone.

CELEBRATION COUNT DOWN!

Whether counting down the days until Christmas, summer vacation, a birthday, or any other highly-anticipated event, waiting can be tough for kids. (Grandmas, too!) A count-down chain is a great visual aid that's fun to make—and pull apart! Cut strips out of construction paper (about 1 1/2 inches wide and 6 to 7 inches long), one for each day you'll be counting down. Tape or glue the strips together in linking circles to make a chain. At one end of the chain, tape or staple a postcard or picture the grandkids have drawn representing the Big Event. Tape the finished chain somewhere everyone can see it. Every evening at bedtime, have grandkids take turns carefully tearing one link off of the chain.

INDOOR SNOWBALL FUN

Any season is the right time to play with a little faux snow!

- Have a snowball fight with marshmallows.

- Crumple white tissue paper into snowballs and toss them into an empty box or laundry basket, taking a step backward with every throw.

- Stack marshmallows to look like snowmen. Stick toothpicks in for arms. Set them about an inch apart each other on a paper plate. Then, have Grandma put them in the microwave, turn it on, and let the snowmen "joust" each other. The first snowman that falls over loses.

SNOW SHOW

When snow is falling outside, bundle up the grandkids—and bring along a black sheet of construction paper and a magnifying glass. Lay the paper on the ground. Then, take a closer look at the patterns in each snowflake that falls on the paper. Look quickly before they disappear!

RAIN, RAIN DON'T GO AWAY

When the rain refuses to go away, turn it into a game. Make a homemade rain gauge. Take an empty plastic prescription bottle, label removed. With a permanent market, mark lines up the side at 1/4-inch intervals, starting at the bottom. Secure a popsicle stick to the side of the bottle with a rubber band. Stick the popsicle stick in the ground, placing the rain gauge in a place the grandkids can see from a window. Check the gauge every morning to see how much it rained the previous day.

COLOR DAY

Choose a color and try to incorporate it into your day. For example, you and your child could wear clothes for that color, paint a picture using that color, and eat foods that are that special color.

SET UP A NATURE CORNER

Whenever you take a walk, have your grandchildren look for things that are interesting to them, such as a special leaf, rock, pine cone, acorn, or feather. Back home, use a shirt box to make a "nature corner" where these favorite treasures can be kept and looked at again and again.

GETTING TO KNOW YOU

Prepare a list of questions, such as "Who is your best friend?" "What is your favorite color?" "What is under your bed?" "What food do you really hate?" "What is the best thing that ever happened to you?" and other topics. Then take turns asking your grandchildren each question. You might be surprised at the answers! Allow them to ask you the questions too. You will all enjoy getting to know each other better.

Riddle Dee Dee

Why didn't the hot dog star in the movies?

HEARTFELT THANKS

Why wait until Thanksgiving to talk about gratitude? Help your grandkids get a better picture of how much they have to be thankful for every day of the year. Help them brainstorm all of the little "gifts" they receive each day, such as food, a bed to sleep in, clothing, hugs, etc. Then, have them draw a picture of all of the good things in their lives. On the back, help them write a Thank You card to God. At bedtime, read their Thank You note aloud. You can also help them turn it into a prayer.

Riddle Dee Dee

What did the sock say to the foot?

ST. PATRICK'S DAY EGGS

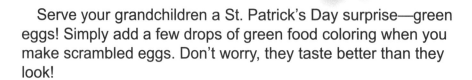

Serve your grandchildren a St. Patrick's Day surprise—green eggs! Simply add a few drops of green food coloring when you make scrambled eggs. Don't worry, they taste better than they look!

HAPPY NEW YEAR!

You don't have to stay up until midnight to have a New Year's Eve party. Shred or cut up construction paper to make confetti. Make party hats by folding a piece of paper into a cone shape and taping it closed, then having kids decorate it any way they like. Serve cheese and crackers and glasses of sparkling cider for a New Year's toast. Then count down the seconds – 10, 9, 8, 7, 6, 5, 4, 3, 2, 1 – and toss your confetti in the air as you shout, "Happy New Year!"

MEMORY GAME

Here's an old favorite worth reviving! Put a variety of easily recognizable objects on the table. Then cover them up and see how many objects your grandkids can recall. Start with three objects and keep adding things until your grandkids' memories can't hold anymore!

Riddle Dee Dee

How do rabbits travel?

HANDPRINT WREATHS

Make a special holiday wreath from your grandchildren's own hands! Place a piece of green construction paper on some newspaper. Spread green fabric paint over your grandchild's hands and have them make handprints in a circle to create a wreath pattern. After the paint dries, draw in a red bow and some red dots for berries.

MAKE LUMINARIAS

You will need brown paper lunch bags, sand, and votive or small candles. Encourage children to decorate the outside of the bag with holiday scenes. Older children can cut out designs with scissors. Then fill each bag with about one inch of sand. Set the candle into the sand. Then place the luminarias outside (along the front sidewalk in a good spot) and light the candles for a beautiful holiday light effect.

PATRIOTIC PUZZLES

Scramble the letters of American-themed words, such as the names of the presidents, states, or national monuments. Write the scrambled words down and challenge your grandchildren to figure out each word. You can also challenge them to see how many smaller words they can create out of the words "American," Fourth of July," "independence," or other patriotic words.

BASEBALL CARD GAME

You can play baseball using a regular deck of cards.

1. Draw a baseball diamond on a piece of paper.
2. Use coins, paper clips, or other markers for the players.
3. Have paper and pencil handy to keep score.
3. Shuffle a deck of cards. The first player (the pitcher) deals one card at a time to the second player (the batter). The batter moves his players around the diamond depending on which card he draw. (See chart below.)
4. After the batter strikes out, walks, or gets a hit, he or she uses a marker to stand for the next batter. Player continues to draw cards until he or she reaches three outs, just like in a real baseball game.
5. Next, the batter becomes the pitcher and deals cards to player #2, who is now the batter.
6. Play continues for nine innings.

2 of any suit—Strike	10 of any suit—Foul ball
3 of any suit—Ball	Jack or Queen of any suit—Fly out
4 of any suit—Strike	King of any suit—Ground out
5 of any suit—Ball	Ace of Clubs—Single
6 of any suit—Strike	Ace of Diamonds—Double
7 of any suit—Ball	Ace of Hearts—Triple
8 of any suit—Strike	Ace of Spades—Home Run
9 of any suit—Ball	Optional: Add one Joker to the deck to stand for a Grand Slam

ALL SEASON CELEBRATION TREE

After Christmas, when artificial tabletop trees are on sale, pick one up for the grandkids. Each month, figure out how you can all decorate it in a way that celebrates the month ahead. Here are a few "ornament" ideas to get your started:

JANUARY—paper snowflakes; cotton ball "snow balls; slips of paper with New Year's Resolutions written on them.

FEBRUARY: Valentines; paper hearts; photos of people you love; anything red.

MARCH: shamrocks; leprechauns; little paper "rain" umbrellas and rainbows; tiny rubber duck bath toys.

APRIL: marshmallow candy bunnies; hand-drawn Easter eggs; April Fool's Day silliness.

MAY: photos of Mom; thank you notes for Mom; "coupons" for Mom of favors and chores the grandkids promise to do the entire month of May.

JUNE: tiny birds and plastic flowers; ice cream cones (decorated to the hilt!).

JULY: anything red, white, and blue; little flags; fake firecrackers; stars.

AUGUST: sunglasses; hand-drawn flip-flops; photos from summer vacation; sea shells.

SEPTEMBER: tiny paper books (titled with your grandchildren's favorite stories); fun pencils; fall leaves (real or hand-drawn); apple shapes.

OCTOBER: jack-o-lantern faces drawn on orange circles of paper; ghosts made out of white tissue paper with a ping-pong ball held in place by a rubber band.

NOVEMBER: slips of paper listing things your grandkids are thankful for; candy corn; "thumbprint" turkeys.

DECEMBER: mini elf hats; stars; Christmas ribbon and bows; animals you'd find in a manger scene; handmade Christmas ornaments; slips of paper for Santa to read, including your grandkids' wish list AND thanks for memorable gifts they've received in the past!

ROCK ZOO

Whether you purchase rocks in a bag from a craft store or have your grandchildren gather them from a nearby park or their own backyard, rocks make an excellent canvas for creativity. If you're using rocks gathered in the "wild," rinse any dirt off of them and let them dry before you begin. Next, gather together an assembly of different craft supplies: googly eyes, pipe cleaners, buttons, small shells, beads, bottle caps, sunflower seeds, small stickers, paint or markers, and glue. Decide which animals you want to include in your zoo. Help your grandkids figure out which rocks look most like the animals they're going to become. Then, go to work! Paint, glue, and use plenty of imagination! If you want to keep the rock animals looking nice for a longer time period, you may want to coat them with a decoupage sealant. If you still have time and energy, why not turn old shoeboxes into cages and enclosure for your menagerie? Then, all that's left to do is help your grandkids take their dolls or stuffed animals on a field trip to the zoo.

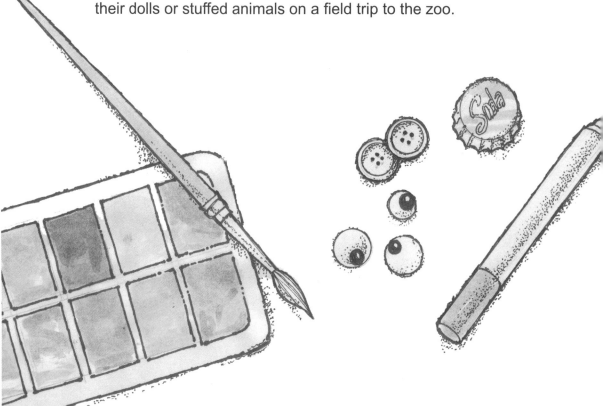

MAKE A PILLOWCASE COSTUME

Use markers to draw a superhero or other logo on an old pillowcase. Cut a hole in the seam at the closed end of the pillowcase so it can fit over your head, and cut the side seams to make arm holes.

Riddle Dee Dee

What runs but cannot walk?

A PASSION FOR FASHION

Put together a box of used clothing (from your own closet or a thrift store). The wilder, the better! Add some costume and accessory odds and ends, such as sunglasses, hats, costume jewelry, a fake nose and glasses, a pirate patch, gloves, a play tiara, clown nose, etc. Give your grandkids three minutes to put on a costume, then start some music and have them give you a private fashion show. Take plenty of pictures on your phone to share with them—and with Mom and Dad. Then, have them change and start all over again—or put on a play, starring the characters they've created. Another idea is to have a Harvest costume fashion show and award prizes to the scariest, silliest, fanciest, prettiest, and weirdest costumes! You could even have a parade.

REVISIT THE GOOD OLD DAYS!

There are plenty of simple games that have gone out of fashion over the years but are still lots of fun to play. Help your grandkids take a peek into your childhood by acquainting them with activities such as hopscotch, jacks, double-dutch jump rope, Tic-Tac-Toe, hide and seek, Bingo, elastic jump rope (aka: Chinese jump rope), hula hoops, and pick-up-sticks—just to name a few! How many more can you remember?

Riddle Dee Dee

What kind of glasses do spies wear?

FRUITY COOKIE PIZZA

Here's a cool pizza for a hot day! Prepare this crust for the kids. Thinly slice one package of refrigerated sugar cookie dough into circles and place them on a pizza pan or stone. Press them together until there are no holes in the "pizza crust." Bake according to package directions. Blend 8 oz. of softened cream cheese, 1/4 cup sugar, and 1/2 tsp. vanilla together until smooth. Let the kids help spread over cooled sugar cookie crust. Let them top the pizza with their favorite fruit, sliced and placed in a circular pattern. Meanwhile, make the glaze. Dissolve 2 1/2 Tbsp. cornstarch in 1/2 cup cold water. Add 1 cup orange juice, 1/4 cup lemon juice, and 1 cup sugar to cornstarch mixture. Heat in a small saucepan over low heat until thick. Cool, then spoon over fruit. Refrigerate for at least 1 hour. Cut into wedges and serve. Serves 8 to 10.

NO BAKE CHRISTMAS TREE ORNAMENTS

This year, start a new holiday tradition. Have each grandchild make and date an ornament for their tree— or yours! Here's an easy recipe for a non-edible dough that makes sturdy, keepsake ornaments. In a medium saucepan, bring 1 1/2 cup water to a boil, then remove from the heat. Stir in 2 cups of salt and 1 cup of cornstarch. Return to low heat and cook until the dough thickens, becoming difficult to stir. Pour dough onto wax paper. When cool, knead dough until smooth. Roll dough to about 1/8 inch thick. Now, have the kids join you and choose their favorite shapes to cut from cookie cutters. Poke a hole in the top of each ornament with a toothpick, widening it enough to later insert a length of ribbon or string. Move the ornaments somewhere out of the way where they can dry for 2 to 3 days, such as the top of the refrigerator or dryer. When ready, let the kids paint with acrylic paints and allow to dry. Paint the year on the back, if desired. Tie a string or ribbon through the hole on each ornament. Hang and enjoy for years to come!

GRANDKID TIMES...

A journal of memorable moments

_____

_____

_____

_____

_____

_____

_____

_____

FROM THE MOUTHS OF BABES...

Sweet and funny things my grandkids said

_____

_____

_____

_____

_____

_____

_____

FUN AND LAUGHTER...

Things that cracked us up

_____

_____

_____

_____

LOVING LEARNING...

Discoveries by my brilliant grandkids

_____

_____

_____

_____

SO CREATIVE...

Projects and play time they enjoyed the most

_____

_____

_____

_____

_____

GOOD EATS...

Favorites. And not so favorite.

_____

_____

_____

_____

_____

CELEBRATIONS...

Ways we celebrated special days

_____

_____

_____

_____

_____

A GRANDMA HOLDS HER GRANDCHILD'S HAND
FOR JUST A LITTLE WHILE ...
BUT SHE'LL BE WRAPPED AROUND THAT LITTLE
PINKIE FOREVER.